JUSTIN AND RUDY'S EXCELLENT IT ADVENTURE

By

Michael Acton, PMP, ITIL© Expert

Edited by Lew Kelsey & Kelly Nietubyc

About the Author:

Dr. Michael Acton is an ITIL© Expert and Project Management Professional (PMP) and has been involved with IT Service Management for many years. He wrote his doctoral dissertation on IT Service Management within a government entity espousing a small baby step methodology versus the sometimes used "Big Bang" approach. Michael Acton has written other non-IT related fiction; and in doing so, he has attempted to build a bridge between the often confusing IT world and the traditional fiction story. "Justin and Rudy's Excellent IT Adventure" links IT Service Management concepts to the contemporary fiction world.

Preface

Why yet another book on IT Service Management? Haven't there already been something like a zillion books written on the subject? Well, yes. As a matter of fact there have been. Unfortunately, many IT books are "dry as dust" I'm sad to say yet obviously I enjoy the subject. This book differs with most of the other books in that it attempts to weave IT concepts into a story. The fundamental problem with managing IT is that it usually does well in board rooms and back offices but often fails where the rubber meets the road…often flying off into a ditch by the side of the road never to be pulled out. In fact, in today's challenging fiscal times, IT Service Management is like the Jehovah's Witness of IT concepts…left standing on the company's porch but seldom invited in. This begs the question, "Should this practice be invited into our already crowded home of seemingly endless IT practices, or left standing on the porch, or abandoned by the side of the road altogether?"

Okay, you're going to hate me for this, but if I gave you the answer to this question now (at least my answer to the question), you wouldn't read the rest of the book. So, we need to build up the suspense just a bit. I'm going on the premise that most who consider reading this book do so because they have only a cursory understanding of its concepts and possible benefits. Honestly, if you're well versed in IT Service Management or have been involved as a Project Manager for any medium to large scale deployment of the concepts, this book probably won't provide much added value…although you will miss out on getting to know Justin Smith and his co-worker, Rudy as they journey through just such a challenging endeavor.

So, we're going to follow Justin Smith on his quest to answer the question, "Is IT Service Management really worth your time and effort?" You see, Justin works for a large insurance company that has its own internal IT department…granted an IT department with issues and in some level of disarray. Justin has become the "go to" guy in the IT department due in large part because he's been there longer than most of his counterparts. He is outgoing, approachable (unlike some of the IT folks in the department), and he's one of the few IT people that have a certification in the subject. Early one morning before Justin starts work, he's going to get an unexpected visit that will set his quest in motion.

It Was a Bad Morning for a Cup of Coffee

Justin usually liked to stop into the company cafeteria early in the morning before his shift started. He knew he would be in for another long day of employees calling him with their computer problems needing him to drop whatever he was doing to assist them. For lack of a better term, Justin was one of five "Desk Side Support" technicians that essentially fixed any problem an employee had with their computers. Many of the problems experienced by the employee, Justin had seen before and he was extremely good at walking the employee through the process of fixing the issue; but there were other times when Justin would need to go to the customer to fix the problem himself. On this morning, while he was drinking his mocha and reading the news on his smart phone, an unexpected visitor came to the company cafeteria...looking for Justin.

"Excuse me, but you're Justin, aren't you?" A commanding voice stated.

Looking up from his phone Justin immediately realized the person standing in front of him was the company CIO (we'll call him Jackson Jones). Justin looked up and recognized Mr. Jones from his photo in the lobby of the building, but he couldn't understand how Mr. Jones knew who he was.

"Mind if I sit down?" Mr. Jones inquired, already pulling out the chair opposite Justin.

"Not at all, sir."

"I understand you're the main guy down in my IT department." Mr. Jones started, breaking the ice.

Justin wasn't the main guy as much as he was one of the most experienced techs in the IT department.

"I'm not sure about that, sir." Justin said, now realizing some of the others in the cafeteria were looking in his direction, obviously curious why the CIO would be having a conversation with Justin.

"I don't want to take up your time..." Mr. Jones said pointing to Justin's coffee. "...but I've been told you have some background in IT Service Management."

"Yes. I have the basic certification. I got it on my own a few years ago." Justin responded.

"Great. So I was in a symposium last week and many IT managers were discussing the benefits of it...sounded promising.

What I need from you since you're one of the few around here with some actual knowledge of the subject is: Is IT Service Management worth our time and effort for our company?"

"Well…" Justin stammered, trying to come up with an acceptable response to such an open-ended question.

"Stop right there…I don't need an answer right now…come to my office on Wednesday afternoon and we can discuss it.

"Great." Justin sarcastically thought, catching a bit of a reprieve.

Mr. Jones got up to depart shaking a few hands as he headed out of the cafeteria. All eyes remained on Justin; continuing to wonder why the CIO sought him out. At that point, Rudy, who works Desk Side Support with Justin came over to Justin's table.

"What the heck did the big man want with you?" Rudy inquired.

"He wants me to tell him if I think any IT Service Management concepts are beneficial for our company." Justin replied, still surprised by the encounter. "It's been a few years since I had that class, I don't remember much about it. I need to get back to my cube and do a little research." Justin said.

"I'm headed that way too, I'll walk with you." Rudy responded.

Both headed out of the cafeteria and down to the basement where their adjoining cubes were located. Both expected to have more than a few employee voice messages waiting for them on a typical Monday morning. When they got to their cubicles, both looked at their phones to check for messages...Rudy had 3 and Justin only 2.

"Hey you mind if I send you a couple of my messages to handle? I have to do a little research." Justin inquired to Rudy.

"Sure. Let me know if I can help with the stuff. I wouldn't mind being the CIO's buddy too." Rudy joked.

History and Overview...boring stuff

Justin searched through his desk to find the old training documents. Buried at the bottom of one of his file drawers, he found what he was looking for...one of the training manuals he used when he was studying for the certification exam. He almost wanted to yell "Eureka!" as he pulled it from the drawer; but he refrained. He leafed through the manual stopping at the short section that discussed the history of IT Service Management. He figured this would be good information to know for the meeting with Mr. Jones on Wednesday.

Since the late 1980's when the concepts that were to be known as Information Technology Service Management were first introduced, organizations have realized the benefits of a standardized framework, but many organizations are unable to find a way to incorporate this framework into their day to day operational business processes. Since this covers such a breadth and depth of IT services, and because it takes an academic slant, it is often regarded by IT users as overly cumbersome to implement. The framework is also sometimes regarded as too generic to be useful for off-the-shelf usage and implementation...

"Blah, Blah, Blah." Justin thought. He skipped down until he came to the specific part on the History.

One of the prevailing myths is that there is no need to have an understanding of the history and origins of the concepts prior to undertaking efforts to implement it within an organization. This statement could not be further from the truth. To fully understand any subject and how to properly use it, it is imperative to have an understanding of its impetus and the reasons behind its existence and development. This is not possible without a basic understanding of the history of the subject.

When technology departments first began to be added to businesses and organizations in efforts to improve the customer's experience through technology, most of these businesses had little understanding for how these IT departments actually impacted the business and ultimately the customers. Most of the employees that made up these departments were skilled in the technical side of the department with little knowledge of management or understanding of the business they were supporting. Over time, managers began to become concerned with the overall efficiency of their IT infrastructures and its ability to support their customers. This concern lead to a number of initiatives to improve IT efficiency which included brainstorming sessions, focus groups, and work simplification programs. Although bringing improved efficiencies to the IT department was a valued business goal, often these initiatives faded almost before they started.

It is not uncommon for an organization's newly appointed leader to institute some form of improvement initiative when appointed to their position. Often once this leader departs the organization, so does that initiative. Other times, initiatives are begun without the full support of organizational leadership or a primary supporter with enough influence to sustain the effort. Without this support, there is little opportunity for the initiative to take a foothold within the organization.

Business competition can often supply the spark for an initiative to take root. In the late 1980s a series of process management initiatives took hold in American industry. These initiatives focused on methods to improve the quality of products and services an organization offered to its customers. Continuous Process Improvement (CIP) and Total Quality Management (TQM) are two early examples. Only limited use of these (and others) is still in use today. The comings and goings of such initiatives

suggests that these programs are easy to start, difficult to sustain,

and usually have a short life cycle. What makes IT Service

Management different from other similar initiatives?

Perhaps the most significant reason why it has not

only stood the test of time but has begun to flourish may be its

linkage to management. Whereas service management has emerged

from so many varied points of view it has often been difficult to settle

on an established definition that the world would fully embrace. In

his book, "At America's Service," Karl Albrecht seemed to capture

the basics of the concept when he stated, "Service management is a

total organizational approach that makes quality of service, as

perceived by the customer, the number one driving force for the

operations of the business."

It was starting to all come back to Justin now. He
remembered that it was a customer focused approach and that was
what interested him in the certification in the first place. He
continued reading…

It is commonly accepted that its history can be traced back

to the middle 1980's in Great Britain. The British government realized that its vast bureaucracy had become more dependent on computers and technology to process large quantities of data necessary to support their citizens and customers. The British government also realized that the more dependent they became on these computer systems, the job they were doing in providing reliable services to their users dramatically declined. What had been put into place to streamline operations (computer systems) had ultimately created additional burdens and caused existing processes to become less efficient.

In 1986, the British government authorized the Centralized Telecommunications and Computing Agency (CTCA) to sponsor a program to promote improved efficiencies in the management of IT services. The agency issued a call to the public, private, and academia sectors of the country to come forward with ideas and to establish a best practice framework for managing within the IT environment. The result of this effort was the publication of over 40 books in 1989 that became the first version of the concept. This was a monumental effort to be sure; however, to ask the IT practitioner to fully understand 40 books prior to being able to utilize the framework was less than realistic. It was clear from the outset that *version one was only the beginning and that it would need to undergo additional transformations prior to being a framework that the practitioner could fully embrace.*

By the mid 1990's, the volumes that made up version one had swelled to 60 and had become extremely unwieldy. Based largely on input from an organization formed in the Netherlands called the Information Technology Service Management Forum (itSMF), work began to condense the 60 books into something more manageable. The end result of version 2 (V2) was a sizable reduction of the material from 60 books to only seven. The texts that comprised V2 were: Service Support; Service Delivery; Security Management; Application Management; Information & Communication Technology (ICT) Infrastructure Management; Planning to Implement Service Management; and The Business Perspective. This was a significant departure from version one in that the volume of material was vastly reduced. Furthermore, the bulk of the practical material was contained within only two books; Service Support and Service Delivery. In fact, these two books contained the bulk of the material on which certification was based.

In 2000, a number of related events occurred. In Great Britain, the CCTA merged into the Office of Government Commerce (OGC) therein cementing the idea that IT should serve the business and not the other way around. Microsoft became one of the first American companies to embrace IT Service Management and the publication of the first of the V2 books (Service Support) were two other major events to start the new millennium. It was a relatively short period of time before it was realized that the concept required another major revision.

Version 3 retained the IT focus on providing services to customers and users; however included the concept that services can best be explained and utilized within the context of a lifecycle. This change's most significant contribution was the introduction of services as a lifecycle. V3 describes the service as having five distinct stages throughout its life. They include Service Strategy, Service Design, Service Transition, Service Operation, and Continual Service Improvement.

It was almost exclusively a European concept until the turn of the century when it began to make some traction in the United States. There have been many theories as to why the United States lagged behind the European community in its adoption. Additionally, many scholars have speculated as to which triggers actually spawned its emergence into the United States early in the 21st century.

The global war on terrorism has often been listed as one impetus to the interest in IT as a service within organizations in the United States. The threat of failed infrastructure was never greater in the minds of business leaders than after the 9/11 attacks. A single threaded data center, if wiped out, could require thousands of man-hours to restore and cost a considerable amount of money and business capital to bring the business back to a pre-attack status. Part of the V2 methodology details continuity planning strategies, which was of particular importance to business leaders post 9/11.

A second trigger for the advancement in its interest in the United States was the further globalization of the world economy. During this time, many American companies decided to open up data centers and other business units in overseas locations. In doing so, many of these business leaders saw the benefits of their European counterpart's use of the processes and this sparked their interest. Much of what was observed was brought back and the news of its success overseas began to spread within the American corporate environment. Certainly arguments suggesting other triggers impacted its initiation in the U. S. are just as valid, the two listed above are presented here only to illustrate the kind of event or situation that need be present to influence its use in the United States.

The adage, "you must know where you have been before you can know where you are going" is a testament to the importance of understanding the history of a subject. This is as true for IT Service Management as it is for any subject. It would be exceedingly difficult to implement without a thorough understanding of where it came from and how it has transformed into what it is today.

"How are you coming over there?" Rudy shouted from his cube.

It was then that Justin realized it had been 45 minutes since he first sat down to read/scan over the history in the manual and his coffee was now gone.

"Pretty good. I think I have a pretty good handle on the history stuff. I need a refresh of the whole Service Management

Lifecycle and Processes…but it's all starting to come back to me."
Justin shouted back to Rudy.

"Any more calls you want me to take?" Rudy inquired.

Justin looked at his phone and saw three more voice
messages.

"Yeah, three more coming your way. Lunch is on me today."
Justin said to Rudy.

First on Justin's list was a search of some basic data on the
Lifecycle and Service Strategy. He leafed through the manual a bit
before resorting to the table of contents. He found what he was
looking for.

What's Service Strategy all about anyway?

Justin noticed this graphic in the manual and he immediately recalled that everything revolved around the strategy part.

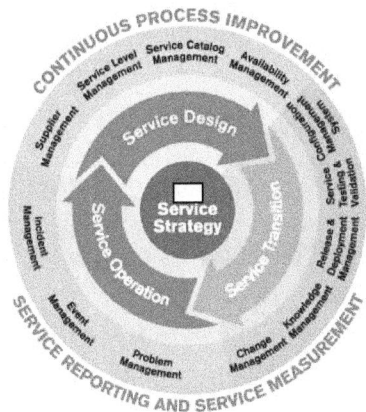

"Yeah, I remember this." Justin whispered to himself. He scanned the section on Service Strategy…

Service Strategy serves as the centerpiece of the lifecycle. Service Strategy delivers guidance in developing service management as a strategic resource for the business. This phase of the lifecycle helps the organization develop a usable strategy that can be incorporated into their business strategy. Strategy is often related to the military world where in this context the application and distribution of resources are used to accomplish a particular objective of a military plan or to defeat an adversary. It is not much different in the IT Service Management arena. The goal of Service

Strategy is to identify the competition (adversary) and to compete with them by distinguishing oneself from the rest by delivering superior performances. IT Service Strategy addresses a number of key concepts that aid the organization in accomplishing this. A large part of a Service Strategy is determining whether a service provides value to the business/organization or not. Customers value IT service when they see a distinct relationship between that IT service and the business value they need to produce. The level of value the customer perceives from the IT service is made up of two separate but related components: Utility and Warranty.

With regards to IT services, utility is fitness for purpose and warranty is fitness of use. The service customer or user's perception regarding utility is derived based on whether the service has a positive effect on the performance of tasks associated with a desired outcome. The removal or lessening of constraints on performance is also viewed positively by customers. Warranty happens when a service is available when needed, in enough capacity, dependable in regards to continuity, and secure. If a customer were evaluating a data storage service to determine if it created value to the business, utility would be evaluated in terms of data storage performance and any possible performance constraints. At least positive performance or lack of constraints results in the service being fit for purpose. It does not pass the value test until it passes the warranty test as well. If the proposed data storage service is available when needed, have the required capacity, dependability, and security it is deemed fit for use. So, as perceived by the customer, if the service is both fit for purpose and fit for use than it is deemed to be a value creating service.

IT service customers must have services fit for purpose and use. Service providers must offer services that create value for their customers. Purchasing value (by the customer) and producing and offering value (by the service provider) are cornerstone strategic outcomes for both parties and are a foundation of Service Strategy. Within this lifecycle phase, there are three processes that will be discussed: Financial Management, Service Portfolio Management, and Demand Management.

"Hey Rudy…you busy?"

"I've got a few minutes." Rudy said poking his head up from his cube so he could see Justin.

"You know anything about the strategy our company uses to make IT decisions? You remember last year when we had that big computer swap out for every employee…there must have been some kind of strategic decision that aligned somehow to the business strategy." Justin inquired.

"Good question. I just remember we got a list of PCs to swap out periodically and we had a week to get it done. A couple of weeks later another list fell out of the sky. Maybe there was a strategy behind it, but I remember lots of employees complaining when I came up to swap out their box."

"Yeah, me too…" Justin chimed in. "…lots of folks had programs on their local machines. When I swapped them out, they lost a tool they needed to do their jobs."

"Well, in that case, it doesn't sound very strategic to me."

"Me neither. Sounds like some big wig decided it would be a good thing to do, without looking at how it impacted the employees directly. Okay, let me look at Service Design in this manual."

A Poor Service Design = A Poor Customer Experience

Once again, Justin turned his attention to the manual, familiar now with its layout, he quickly turned to the Service Design section.

In keeping with the lifecycle approach to managing IT services; once the strategy has been fully addressed, it now comes time to design these services. This phase is concerned with developing appropriate IT services that meet the needs of current and future customers. Included within this design phase would be the architecture, processes, policy, and documentation of these services. The actual design goal is to meet the current and future business requirements of the prospective customers of these services.

The Service Design phase begins when a request for a new or modified service is received by the IT provider from a customer. Ultimately, at the end of the design phase, a service solution must be presented that meets all customer requirements. This design solution could be anything from a simple software program that provides a new or modified functionality for a small group of users to a new building complete with a massive IT infrastructure capable of supporting hundreds of employees. Regardless of the design scope, the end result is the same. The design solution should deliver exactly what is specified in the customer requirement—no more

functionality than was requested and no less.

A design that exceeds customer requirements risks delivering
a service that does not meet the needs of the customer at an
increased cost to the service provider. A design that falls short on
delivering what the customer requested causes rework at the expense
of the service provider and delays in the deliverable to the customer.
This can also result in a less favorable opinion of the service
provider by the customer that could result in future lost business
opportunities for the provider. It is clear the service design should
match the customer requirement exactly; as this produces the
greatest benefit to both parties.

Justin immediately thought of the PC swap and how this effort certainly didn't meet with all the customer's requirements...if you assume our own employees were also our IT customers. Those that lost functionality as a result of the PC swap were a victim of poor Service Design.

"Why couldn't special PCs for employees that needed a certain tool have been designed and built based on the customer requirements?" Justin asked in a low voice; obviously referring to

the PC swap out again.

Don't Just Kick it Over the Fence...Transition it.

Justin was starting to put the pieces of these service management concepts together in his mind and realized that what his company does on a day to day basis wasn't aligned to it at all...really wasn't aligned to much of anything. Before going to lunch, he wanted to check out the Service Transition section quickly, although he felt pretty comfortable with the material.

With the strategy and design of a service addressed, it is now time to put the newly developed service into operation. But a service cannot be placed into the operational environment of a business immediately after being developed. It must first be transitioned into the operational environment. Why? To answer this question all that is needed is to ask virtually any IT operations individual. IT history is filled with incidents of service developers and designers deploying a new service without regards to a transitional period. The end result of this "tossing a new service over the fence to operations" is filled with potential dangers. Some of these dangers might be:
--implementing a new IT service that is replacing an older service which has not been properly decommissioned.

--*Service Desk personnel not being trained on how to respond to user inquiries on the new service.*

-- *Users not trained on how to utilize the new service.*

--*What impact does the new service have on existing services?*

These are just a small sample of some of the potential problems and issues that may emerge if a new or modified service is placed into operation without being properly transitioned into the live business environment. Service Transition phase of the lifecycle attempts to provide some structure in moving this service into the operational arena of the business; thereby minimizing potential problems when doing so.

This can be accomplished by ensuring the service meets the requirements of the service specifications, by supporting the existing change process (if there is one) of the business, and by reducing variations in the performance and known errors of new/changed services. These are all goals of Service Transition and highlight its role within the overall process. Prior to addressing this lifecycle phase and its processes further, it is important to understand the phase's value to the business.

To that end, within the Service Transition phase, the Change Management, Service Asset & Configuration Management, Release & Deployment Management, and Knowledge Management processes can reduce the likelihood the business will experience any adverse impact to the deployment or modification to a service. Perhaps the most significant impact to the business is change itself. All businesses that rely on IT services are faced with making some form of change to their IT infrastructure at some point. Understanding the impact these changes can have to customers and end users is critical.

"Rudy, are you ready for some lunch?" Justin asked, rubbing his eyes with the palms of his hands.

Rudy responded eagerly, "If you're still buying…you bet." He popped into Justin's cubicle; his mouth watering with the thought of a free meal.

"You don't mind if I run a few thoughts about this stuff by you while we eat?" Justin inquired.

"Not if you don't mind me answering with my mouth full of free food." Rudy answered smiling.

"Works for me…let's go." Justin said closing up the Service

Management manual and pushing it to the side.

Plans Devised Over Lunch

Justin and Rudy told their three co-workers they were taking a working lunch in the cafeteria and would be gone an hour or so. No one seemed to have a problem with that as they had already heard that the CIO had asked Justin to look into something for him. They figured Justin had magically become the CIO's pet. To question what he did and when he did it didn't seem wise…plus, for a Monday it surprisingly wasn't all that busy. So Justin and Rudy headed to the cafeteria with hundreds of ideas swimming around in Justin's head.

Justin and Rudy both got in line to grab an individual size pizza. Each grabbed a meat lover's pizza and a soft drink and after Justin paid for the food they found a table at the rear of the cafeteria by a window.

"Thanks for lunch." Rudy said as he opened his pizza box to look admiringly at his free meal.

"No problem. Thanks for your help this morning." Justin replied without looking up from his pizza. Rudy noticed the contemplated expression on his friend's face.

"Okay, so what's on your mind?" Rudy asked before taking a bite of his pizza.

"Man, looking over that stuff again…there are so many improvements we can make around here if the boss is really serious about it." Justin said with a sigh.

"Like what?"

"Where do I begin?" Justin said, finally starting to eat his pizza. "Well, take the PC swap out for instance. When I showed up with a new PC and told them I was there to swap out their old one; not a single employee had any idea I was coming. That's a pretty massive change to not give your customers any warning."

"Yeah, and don't forget all the local software we had to load to the new PCs for most of those customers. Why couldn't that have been pre-loaded on certain boxes earmarked for specific customers? That certainly would have made the swap go more smoothly and potentially saved a lot of time." Rudy added, still chomping on his pizza.

"Sounds like you're volunteering to help me with this little quest." Justin said with a smile.

"Hold on there, cowboy. I didn't say that."

"Too late. You are now officially working this effort with me." Justin said.

"Crap, I knew this lunch wouldn't really be free." Rudy smiled; not really upset that Justin had "trapped" him into helping. Rudy had always thought there were better ways of doing things in the IT department; but like most, he just kept his ideas to himself not wanting to make waves. Now he had a chance to not only make the waves, but to go surfing on them. He was all in.

"Another thing...aren't you tired of all those voice messages from customers with complaints? How many 'Mapping a network drive' or 'connect to a network printer' calls do you get in a week?"

"Dozens...all the same problem with the same solution." Rudy replied.

"Exactly. Wouldn't it make better use of everyone's time and effort if employee requests for service were funneled to a "service desk" where some of these simple problems could be addressed at a lower level...and faster?"

"Better yet, like I said, some problems have the same fix over and over again...and most are pretty simple. Why not have a "self-help" posted somewhere so employees can read something and map a network drive without calling anyone in the IT department?" Rudy asked.

"I like the way you think. I wonder if the Network and Server teams have any of the same or similar issues." Justin inquired; referring to the other two sections that made up the company's IT department.

"We should probably speak with Steve about this, don't you think?" Rudy said, referring to Steve Parker, who was the Desk Side Support Supervisor, who supervised Justin and Rudy and the three other DSS technicians. Having been with the company for nearly 30 years, Steve had a wealth of corporate knowledge. For the last year or so, Steve spent his days camped out in his office planning his retirement.

"That's a good idea." Justin replied, seeing they were both nearly done with their lunch. "I have a couple more sections in the manual to go over this afternoon. Maybe you can chat with Steve when we get back downstairs?"

"Yeah, that sounds fine." Rudy said as he rose to get up. Justin followed his lead and both headed back to their basement cubicles, having finished their lunch in record time.

"Let me check my voice messages first and then I'll stick my head in Steve's office to see if he's busy." Rudy mentioned.

"Busy? Yeah, right." Justin said with a chuckle. "I'm going to refresh myself on the Service Operation stuff now…but I kind of feel I'm good on that part of the lifecycle."

Service Operation—Where the Rubber Meets the Road

Back at his desk, Justin opened the Service Operation section in the manual and began to scan.

Service Operation is where the services are actually put into practice for the customer. This is where the benefits that the customers envisioned when the service was purchased are realized (hopefully). Service Operation (SO) is the point in the process where the delivery of the service to the customer takes place by the act of a service provider performing a set of procedures and/or activities. SO is more than just the repetitive execution of a standard set of procedures or activities. All functions, processes and activities are designed to deliver a specified and agreed level of service, but they have to be delivered in an ever-changing environment. This is one of the more challenging aspects of SO; as the business and technology environments change over time, services must continue to be delivered to the business at the agreed levels of service and at an acceptable cost.

Service Operation is consistently challenged to balance the quality of the services delivered versus the costs of those services. For all services being provided, there is an agreed level of services that is promised. The challenge is to maintain this level at an optimum cost and resource utilization level. Although this may seem to be a straightforward premise, in the current global economic times, organizations are under severe pressure to increase the quality of service while reducing costs. This may seem like a contradiction in terms; how can quality increase while reducing costs? However, it is possible to increase service quality while reducing costs. Initiation for this goal usually occurs in Service Operation while fully formalized in the Continual Service Improvement phase of the process. Some cost savings initiatives can be done incrementally over time whereas other measures are savings that are realized only once. For example, if there are two similar software tools that do essentially the same thing for the customer; the reduction of one tool will be a one-time cost savings. Additionally, if a service can be provided by a team of four employees versus the current five employee team; this is an incremental savings that will be experienced over time as only four employees are needed instead of five. Another challenge that often falls within the Service Operation's realm is whether the organization is being reactive or proactive in its response to day to day operations of the IT infrastructure.

Regarding an organization's service operations, they can have either a reactive or proactive focus. A reactive organization does not act until some sort of stimulus compels the organization or individual to do so. For example, a Service Desk technician working in the network operations department (OPS) may be monitoring the organization's network health using software tools. The technician may not do anything until an alert is displayed on the screen. At that point, the technician may react by documenting the anomaly and initiating procedures to correct the problem. A proactive organization/individual is always looking for ways to improve the current situation. In a proactive environment, that same technician may be monitoring network bandwidth and making data traffic adjustments to ensure no one path gets overly congested with traffic which would cause a problem. This is an example of being proactive in the service operations arena.

Although there is nothing inherently wrong with an organization being solely reactive in nature, usually proactive behavior is viewed more positively because it enables the *organization to keep a competitive advantage in an ever changing*

environment. One concept to keep in mind is that an organization

that has chosen to be overly proactive can incur considerably more

costs than one which is more reactively focused. Often a balance

must be reached between affordability and either reactive or

proactive operations.

The processes aligned to Service Operation phase of the

overall lifecycle are all aimed to provide structure to the operations

of the IT services being provided to the business/customer by the IT

provider. Those processes include; Incident Management, Problem

Management, Access Management, Event Management, & Request

Fulfillment. Perhaps the most visible process to the end user is

Incident Management, which will be addressed next.

"Incident Management and a Service Desk are what we need

around here." Justin thought as he continued to read through the

text. He decided to skip ahead to the Incident Management process

section. He wanted to read that because he thought it would be of

particular interest to Mr. Jones, when they met later in the week.

The Incident Management process handles all incidents of an

organization. Incidents may be failures, questions, or queries submitted by organizational users or technical staff to a service

desk, or observed through the use of specialized monitoring

software. An incident is defined as an unplanned disruption to an IT

service or a reduction in the quality of that service. The primary

objective of Incident Management is to resume normal operations as

quickly as possible and to minimize the impact on business

processes.

Incident Management entails much more than simply

responding to network outages. A Service Desk is often the function

within an IT department that "owns" all incidents for an

organization. The process flow for handling incidents is briefly

explained here based on a flowchart that appears in the book, IT

Service Management: A Guide for Certification Exam Candidates.

The Incident Management flowchart is included in the Appendix of

this manual for reference.

Justin flipped to the back of the manual to look at the

referenced Incident Flowchart and immediately remembered it from

his training. He tabbed the page in the appendix thinking he would

need to refer to that again later. He continued reading…

An incident is usually elevated by means of a user phone call to the Service Desk, a web user interface ticket created by a user/customer, or from event management software that illustrates an outage of some kind. An incident is not handled until it is known to exist. This is the incident identification step. Next, it must be logged (or registered). This is where a ticket is created in an outage tracking system (such as Remedy or Seibel, for example) to document all relevant information related to the outage. Categorizing the incident is the next step which may highlight what type of incident has occurred. Categories may be based upon the different type of networks or equipment used within the organization. Often how incidents are categorized varies by organization. Priority of the incident must be addressed based on urgency and impact it has on the organization. Priority levels 1 through 4 are often used with 1 being most severe or a major incident. Initial diagnosis occurs when the service desk technician tries to establish what went wrong and how it should be corrected. At this point the technician must determine if the incident can be corrected at their level or whether it must be passed on to a higher skilled technician or engineer for resolution. This is called functional escalation.

Depending on the level of business impact, management escalation may also be necessary. Regardless of which entity corrects the problem, the next step is resolution and recovery where a normal operational state returns and the service desk technician resolves or closes the incident record.

Incident Management is a critical component of Service Operation's efforts to maintain the steady state of normal business operations by resolving issues as quickly as possible by virtually any means necessary. However, in most cases during Incident Management the underlying cause of the incident is not directly addressed.

"Okay, and this is where Problem Management comes in…to discover the underlying cause…or root cause of an incident or group of incidents." He said aloud to himself; realizing that he had retained a better understanding of Service Operation and particularly Incident Management than he initially gave himself credit for.

Someone Always Knows Where the Bones are Buried

Justin saw Rudy heading over to Steve Parker's office. Since he was at a good place to stop in his review of the manual, he decided to catch up to his buddy and join him. When both arrived at Mr. Parker's office, Justin poked his head in and spoke.

"Steve, do you have a couple of minutes?"

"Sure boys, come on in." Steve responded.

Steve Parker was a robust man who had long let his physical appearance go…riding a desk for the majority of his career had taken its toll. But he was friendly and engaging, if not at all motivated at this stage in his career.

"I understand the boss gave you a bit of a task to work on this week?"

"Yes he did." Justin replied.

"You know, that stuff will never work around here. The culture here is stuck in a time-warp. We operate like it's still in the 1970s. That's where everyone's comfort zone is." Mr. Parker started, setting the tone right from the start, and revealing that he already knew what Justin as tasked to do.

"I kind of figured that. But I...I mean we...still have to report back to the CIO later in the week with our thoughts and recommendations."

"So, you got pulled into this too, Rudy?"

"The cost of a free lunch, I'm afraid." Rudy responded patting his friend on the back.

"Well, we would like to ask you a few questions about things in the IT department since you've been with the company for so long." Justin chimed in.

"I'd be happy to tell you what I know, but it will have to wait until tomorrow morning...I'm leaving in a few minutes for a doctor's appointment." Mr. Parker said while starting to power down his computer.

"Yeah, you've been here a long time, I'm sure your insight into how things work around here will be helpful." Rudy said as he and Justin rose to leave.

"Boys..." Steve said in a fatherly tone. "...you know you're going to run into some resistance here, right? Even with the CIO's endorsement for this IT stuff, there are some section heads that are going to be…not very cooperative; assuming the leadership decides to go with whatever recommendation you both come up with."

"Yeah, we understand." Justin replied.

Both headed back to their cubes. Rudy wanted to take care of a few more customer issues before the day ended and Justin wanted to read the last section on Continual Service Improvement, the last of the Lifecycle processes.

CSI—Nothing Stays the Same; All Things Change Eventually

Justin settled in at his desk and found the Continual Service Improvement section in the manual and began to scan it…

Everything is worthy of improvement at some point in its lifecycle. In the 1980s and earlier, if someone wished to compose a letter or write a story; they would often use a typewriter to complete the task. An argument could easily be made that a personal computer with a word processing program installed is nothing more than an improvement on the typewriter. Many years ago the primary mode of transportation was the horse and buggy. The improvement on the horse and buggy was the horseless carriage; otherwise known as the automobile. The point is that all things outlive their useful purpose and must be changed, adapted, or improved upon to remain in a useful state. This is as true for services as it is for the products that we use every day.

IT services exist in order to support the business. So IT services must align and re-align to the changing business needs by making improvements to the IT services that support and often sustain the business strategy. This service improvement is such a critical aspect of IT service management, the concept is considered the fifth and final phase of the overall IT Service Management process.

Continual Service Improvement (CSI) and organizational change are closely tied because in order to make continual improvements a cultural change in organizational mentality is often required. Many CSI initiatives fail because they are unable to achieve this cultural change; and being unable to do so means an organization can become stuck in the status quo without the ability to achieve needed improvements.

Justin noticed a few paragraphs down in the manual where it discussed some critical steps that were developed by a Harvard Professor that would be vital for a company to successfully change. This struck a chord with Justin as he knew that any level of process adoption within the company would prove to be a significant change from the way the company currently conducted business. These steps could prove to be useful, he thought. He read them and marked the page.

--<u>Create a Sense of Urgency</u>—*ask the question "what happens if we do nothing at all and keep the status quo?"*

--_Form a coalition_—usually one person cannot change an entire organization. A small key team with the proper authority and resources can begin making the change.

--_Create a vision_—a good organizational vision helps to create a goal and purpose for CSI.

--_Communicate the vision_—all stakeholders should understand the vision; putting together a communications plan can help.

--_Empower others to act on the vision_—remove obstacles and provide clear direction by setting attainable goals. Supply people with the resources they need.

--_Plan for and create quick wins_—determine what small improvements can be made quickly and successfully. Communicate these successes to the team to build added support.

--_Consolidate improvements and create more change_-- quick wins motivate; medium term improvements provide confidence in the organization's ability to effect change.

--_Institutionalize the change_—Make change acceptance the norm in the organization by:

-Hiring employees with experience in the field of IT management.

-From the outset of a change improvement initiative, utilize work instructions to provide clarity.

-Set up a training effort to provide IT management training.

-Integrate new IT solutions and projects with existing processes.

With that section marked for future reference he continued to scan through the CSI section looking for anything further that might be of use. He found a short section on the Deming Cycle and bookmarked that as well.

The Deming model can be equally applied to aid in implementing an improvement process within an organization or to make improvements within already existing IT services within an organization. The latter is where the primary focus will be. When PDCA (Plan/Do/Check/Act) is used in conjunction with continual improvement of processes and services, the focus is more on the "check" and "act" steps. There are some activities in the "plan" and "do" steps that are addressed; these are not the primary focus.

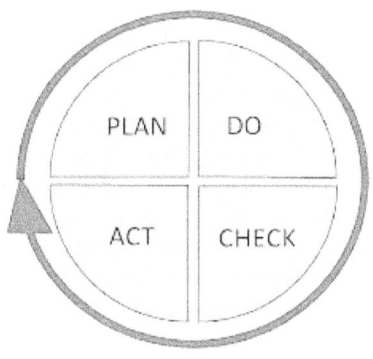

When planning improvement initiatives with IT services

goals must be set at the very outset to ensure everyone understand

the desired end state. Additionally, expected gaps anticipated in

attaining the goal must be identified and addressed if possible. In

the "do" step, it is important to provide a smooth execution of the

process and to eliminate as many obstacles and discrepancies as

possible. During the "check" step of the PDCA, implemented

service improvements are compared to the measures of success

established during the "plan" phase. This comparison determines if

a gap exists between the improvement objectives and the operational

process state. The expected output from the "check" stage is a

recommendation for an improvement. The "act" step requires the

implementing of the actual service and service management

improvements. Project decisions at this stage serve as the input for the next round of the Plan-Do-Check-Act cycle, closing the loop as

input to the next "plan" step.

Justin next noticed the 7 Step CSI process graphic and

bookmarked it as well…

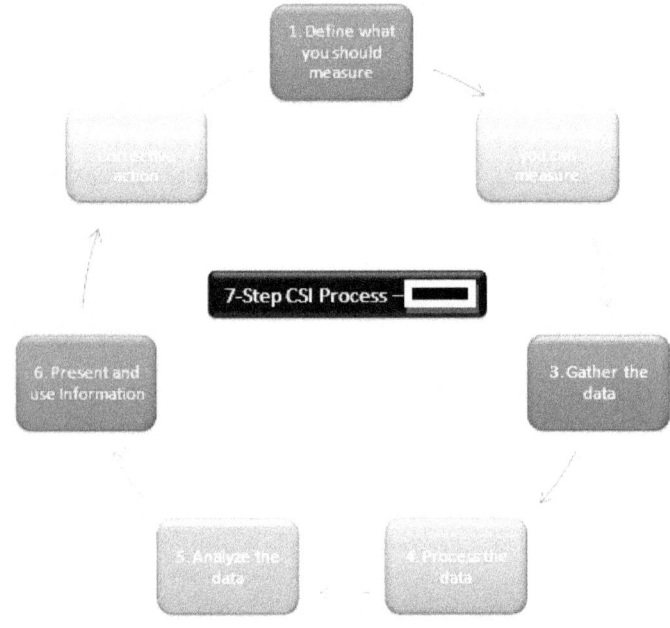

Justin realized that a one day crash course review in these

topics does not an expert make, but he felt better about his

understanding of the concepts than he did when the CIO first

approached him; and felt more prepared and ready for the meeting

later in the week. But there would be more data to gather in order to

make an informed recommendation. For this part, he would need to rely on help from Rudy and whatever data they could get from Steve at tomorrow's meeting in Steve's office.

As Justin was closing up the manual, he overheard what sounded like Rudy closing up for the day.

"Hey, you hanging around for a bit?" Rudy inquired.

"Yeah, I've got a few voice messages in my queue; figured I might as well take care of those if the employee is still around." Justin replied.

"Okay, I'll see you tomorrow." Rudy said as he turned to depart.

As was his usual practice when he had multiple messages, Justin would play them all to see which ones he could knock out quickly…ironically, he thought, after playing the messages there were three customers complaining about connecting to a network printer, one needing a connection to a network server, and two customers needing their passwords reset.

"I'm betting all of these could be issues that could be served by a self-service process…oh well." Justin muttered under his breath as he set to addressing the issues one by one. After nearly 90 minutes, he had all the customer's concerns cleared and his voice mail queue was empty. Justin used the opportunity to call it a day.

He grabbed all his things and headed out; but suddenly turned

around and grabbed the manual to take home with him. He figured

better to have it with him than not; although he didn't plan to

consider the CIO's tasking this evening; but for some reason he

thought it best to keep the manual close at hand.

Home is Where the IT Mind Wanders

Normally, the first thing Justin did when he got home was make something to eat for dinner before catching up on the news on one of the local news channels. As he walked into his tiny one bedroom apartment, he placed the manual on the small kitchen counter, proceeded into the living room and clicked on the television. Then he walked into the kitchen and decided a ham sandwich would suffice for the night's meal. After creating his culinary masterpiece he brought it and a bottle of water into the living room to watch the news.

There was a story about a race car driver being pulled over for speeding…go figure…on the news, but his ability to concentrate on the news was being fractured by thoughts of IT service management. It seemed as though the manual sitting on the counter was calling to him like a smoke detector's periodic beeping imploring its battery to be replaced. Justin occasionally glanced over to the manual and then back to the T.V. in an attempt to refocus…it was no use.

"Damn, I should have just left it at work." He said finally giving in to the temptation to open it up to look for further nuggets that could be used in his search for the questions and answers he would need for the CIO meeting.

He was pretty sure he wanted to bring up the Service Desk idea to the CIO when they met on Wednesday, so he thought his time would be well spent looking over that section of the manual. He pulled out a chair at the counter and began looking for the Service Desk section…

A Service Desk understands that information offers companies strategic advantages and it ensures proper mechanisms are in place for the data to be analyzed, produced and distributed seamlessly. The best Service Desks manage information delivery by utilizing best practices to deliver these services. It is the first contact in an organization for any and all IT questions.

According to IT experts, the definition of a Service Desk is – the single point of contact between users and IT Service Management. Tasks include handling incidents and requests, and providing an interface for other IT management processes. The primary functions of the Service Desk are incident control, lifecycle management of all service requests, and communication with the

customer.

Another definition of Service Desk is a center that provides a

Single Point of Contact (SPOC) between a company's customers,

employees and business partners. The Service Desk is designed to

optimize services on behalf of the business and oversee IT functions.

Thus, a Service Desk does more than making sure IT services are

being delivered at that moment, it manages the various lifecycles of

software packages used to provide critical information flow by

utilizing IT best practices.

These best practices enable an IT service provider to ensure

end user data is being delivered consistently under many different

scenarios. Since the Service Desk is a SPOC it understands there are

many reasons services can be interrupted. A Service Desk has the

means within its hierarchy to monitor and manage each layer of

service from beginning to end.

Justin immediately saw the benefit to leadership and

employees/customers in a Service Desk…including the concept of a

SPOC. If any company leader had a question regarding the health of

their IT systems there would be only one entity to contact instead of the multiple ones currently in use. Plus, Justin figured, for the customers it had always been confusing and frustrating for them to know who exactly to call for a problem. What initially seemed to be a PC problem could turn out to be Network related. This ended up costing customers wasted time on the phone with various members of the IT department. If the customer could make one notification of the problem to the Service Desk and hand the issue off to them…to solve or hand off to the appropriate team to resolve…that would be a solution for everyone.

Justin surmised that Mr. Jones (CIO) would find this concept appealing. He now felt he had enough data on the Service Desk to speak intelligently to the CIO about the benefits of the subject. Still, he wanted to understand more on Problem Management; which to Justin seemed to be a natural flow from Incident Management; and he didn't want to take the chance that Mr. Jones might ask about it. He turned to the section on Problem Management and began to read as the television droned on in the background…

The objective of problem management is to prevent problems and incidents, eliminate repeated incidents and minimize the impact of incidents that cannot be prevented. A problem is defined as the cause of one or more incidents. As an example to differentiate between incidents and problems take a group of e-mail servers that always seem to lock up once a day. Calls from e-mail users to the Service Desk would generate incidents where the Service Desk personnel could use a workaround for this known error to correct the problem. In this example, the workaround might be to reboot the servers. E-mail servers are now back in operation and the incidents can be closed. This does not address the underlying reason why these servers lock up daily. Remember that Incident Management's goal to return to normal operation as soon as possible by virtually any means necessary. Incident Management has done its job. Problem Management is now needed to address the reason these servers have this persistent and repetitive issue. A Problem Management ticket may be generated and assigned to a network engineer to work. In our example, perhaps the engineer may discover that the servers are running with corrupted code that is causing the problem. A change request would be generated to delete the old and update the new code on each server. Resolving this problem has an added benefit in that the previous "daily" incidents *on these servers would be eliminated and make the organization's e-mail service more reliable and robust.*

As soon as a problem solution is found it is to be applied to resolve the issue. But care should be taken to ensure the solution does not negatively impact other services. This is where the Change Management process can play a part in the problem solution implementation to help insure that correcting one problem does not inadvertently create others. As should be understood, Problem Management is greatly dependent on an effective Incident Management process to help identify problems; based on reported incidents, as quickly as possible.

Justin found this section very interesting as he now had a workable example of how Incident/Problem/Change management could work together to minimize recurring incidents, solve a problem; all while reducing risk impact on other services. As much as he would like to push on, the long day of reading the manual, continuing into the evening hours, had made him very tired. He knew he needed to put it aside and get a good night's sleep so he and Rudy could pick up the challenge in the morning. Justin stretched out on the sofa and closed his eyes. With the television on in the

background, he fell into a deep and restful sleep.

Back to the Grind and the Buried Bones

Justin and Rudy met up at the company cafeteria the next morning and both had thoughts about what they wanted to ask Steve. It was clear they were on the same page regarding their questions and concerns. They figured Steve would know if any attempts had ever been made to change how the IT department operated. Since Justin and Rudy worked DSS and didn't really have any insight into the Server or Network teams, they needed to know if those teams are still operating in the same antiquated manner as the DSS team…they suspected they were, but with Steve's nearly 30 years experience within the IT department, they were certain he could confirm and provide specifics.

"So, it seems we're on the same page here in what we feel we need to ask Steve about?" Justin stated after both had briefly compared notes based on what they each thought about the night before.

"Yeah, I think it's pretty straightforward…and I think it won't be much of a surprise in what Steve says." Rudy stated.

"Yeah, I agree, but Steve is too good of a resource not to chat with…otherwise we would be going into the meeting with the CIO with only our assumptions." Justin added.

Rudy nodded agreement.

"Well, grab your coffee. Steve should be in his office now…maybe we can catch him before he starts surfing the internet for that perfect retirement destination." Justin joked, causing Rudy to unexpectedly laugh out loud.

When they got down to Steve's office both were pleased to see Steve there and expecting them.

"Hey guys…come on in. I've been waiting on you." Steve said, apparently anxious to get started.

Justin and Rudy entered and sat down. Justin had a small notebook so he could capture some of what Steve would tell them.

"Okay, where do you want to start?"

"Well, let's start with your career here, if you don't mind. I know you've been my boss since I've been working at DSS, but compared to your 30 years with the company that hasn't been that long…where did you work before?" Rudy chimed in right off the bat; somewhat catching Justin off guard.

"Well, okay. I guess that's as good a place as any to get the ball rolling." Steve confessed. "Let's see...where to start?"

Steve pondered for just a few seconds trying to gather up nearly 30 years of service to the company and put those thoughts into a short conversation.

"Well, like most that started here back when I did...we all started as salesmen. This is an insurance company after all..." Steve said with a pause. "...back then everything was done with paper and pen on company forms. There was an old mainframe computer down in the basement, I think, but no one ever came down here and it was maintained by an off-site contractor. We had no internal IT department like we do now...keep in mind there were no computers on anyone's desk back then...it was typewriters primarily. When individual computers started showing up on employee's desks, there came a need for people to work on them...that's when the unofficial IT department got started. I became a part of the new section that worked on computers and stuff and got out of the sales business and have never looked back. As you guys probably know, the IT department has morphed quite a bit into what it is today and I've seen all the various incarnations first hand. Of course now the IT group comprises us (DSS), the Server Team, the Network Team, and the Voice guys."

"Wow, I forgot that Pete and Mark maintain our phone system." Rudy exclaimed.

"So did I." Justin admitted.

"Well, in a nutshell, that's my story. What other questions do you guys have?" Steve interjected while taking a sip from his coffee cup.

"Are you aware of anything the other IT sections are doing...process wise...that could be transferrable to the other IT departments?" Justin inquired.

"Look, let's cut to the chase to save us all a little time..." Steve interjected. "...for as long as I can remember, there has never been much interaction between the sections of the IT department unless something goes wrong. For example, when multiple computers go down we always get called right?"

Justin and Rudy nodded in the affirmative.

"Well, the Network team never gets involved until we call them. What does that tell you?" Steve said.

"It tells me a couple of things…for one, they don't know when their network stuff is not working and employees don't know to call them directly for something that seems out of scope with DSS responsibility." Rudy responded.

"Who's to say the customers should know that it's a network problem…they shouldn't. That's where a customer Single Point of Contact should come in…a Service Desk, right?" Justin said looking for confirmation from Steve.

"Correct. If you can get the CIO to support any part of this…getting a real Service Desk instituted here would be most beneficial. Along with that you could institute some level of Incident Management." Steve said.

"How does that help?" Rudy inquired.

"Do you keep track of all the customer calls you get?" Steve asked Rudy.

"No…I'm not required to." Rudy answered.

"What about you, Justin?"

"I do keep a spreadsheet and track them…but sometimes I don't add every one I get." Justin confessed.

"Exactly. There is no company or IT policy that says we must keep outage metrics on anything…but the question is, should we and if so, who should capture that data?" Steve asked.

Justin and Rudy could see that Steve had given this IT service management stuff a great deal of thought…more than either of them had given him credit for. They now viewed Steve as more than just someone counting the days until he retired.

"My educated guess is that no one; for the most part, in IT is capturing any viable metrics on outages. I would think that if we had a method to do that, leadership would find some of that data very interesting. For example, how many man-hours do we waste each month doing nothing but resetting someone's network password?" Steve inquired.

"Quite a few." Rudy acknowledged.

"Yeah, and it's so simple the user could do it themselves if they knew how. Rudy and I already talked about a self-help option for some simple things." Justin added.

"Sounds to me like you guys are on the right track; I'm happy to say."

"Where do we go from here?" Justin asked.

"You should see if anyone from the Network, Server, and Voice teams will talk to you about this …just to cover your bases. I suppose most already know you were charged with making a recommendation to the CIO. Don't be surprised to find that some won't want to open up much about their day to day stuff. I'm sure the CIO knows already, but for anything to change for the better around here, there need to be an organizational cultural shift…led and supported from the top down."

"Rudy, see what you can get out of the Server and Network teams and I'll check with the Voice guys." Justin inquired. "I also have a bit more reading in the manual to make sure I have a good understanding of a few other topics."

"Sure…I'll see if I can track them down right now." Rudy said.

"Good Luck, and let me know if you need anything else from me." Steve chimed in.

"Thanks. We appreciate your insight." Justin commented as he and Rudy rose from their chairs to leave.

"Paul is in charge of Pete and Mark on the Voice side of things, right?" Justin inquired as he and Rudy exited Steve's office.

"Yeah, I'm pretty sure." Rudy responded.

"Okay, I'm going to track him down…see what you can find out from the Network and Server guys. I'll meet you back at our desks in about an hour?"

Rudy agreed and both headed off in opposite directions.

The Voice Team—Can You Hear Me Now?

Justin found Paul in a phone closet on the second floor pulling some cabling. Paul, the supervisor for the voice guys, often had to help out when things got busy. Apparently, this was one of those times.

"I bet I know what you want, Justin." Paul stated looking over his shoulder while continuing to work in the phone closet.

Justin and Paul weren't exactly friends, but knew of each other and would exchange pleasantries when they passed in the hallway. But much like the other IT teams, each kept to themselves and worked together only when necessary.

"Yeah, I bet you do. News travels fast around here, I guess." Justin replied.

"Hand me that screwdriver will you? So you want to ask me some questions, do you?" Paul said, while he continued to work in the phone closet. This led Justin to believe this was going to be a short conversation.

"Well, I guess you know what the CIO has asked me to do. Can you tell me a little bit about how your team handles phone outages?" Justin asked trying to break the ice a bit.

"Look, I'm sure you're a good guy and all; and I know you're just trying to do what the CIO asked you to do, but any significant changes to the IT department are not going to go over well…I'm sure that even Steve said that." Paul stated matter-of-factly.

"He did."

Paul didn't say much for what seemed like an eternity; presumably hoping Justin would just walk away. When he didn't Paul spun to face Justin.

"Look, we handle outages in much the same way you do over at DSS, I suspect. Customers with phone issues call me and I make a list and dispense the individual outages to my guys."

"So all requests for service must come through you?" Justin inquired, making certain he understood.

"Yeah, I'm the supervisor of the voice section…why not? Isn't it my call which of my guys works which phone problems?" Paul said beginning to get a bit defensive.

"I suppose so; but what if you're on vacation or are out sick? Who does the outage triage then?"

"That doesn't happen much and frankly most phone issues can wait a few days until I get back…it's the users PCs that are really critical; and that's your job." Paul said with a hint of anger.

"What do you think of the idea of having a central reporting point for any IT related issues customers have…staffed by a team that could perhaps take care of the more simple type of outages your guys work on?" Justin proposed, attempting to draw Paul into the recommendation decision; figuring it would be better if Paul felt he had input into the recommendations to the CIO.

Justin could almost see a light begin to flicker above Paul's head.

"Well, it would be nice to have another team take care of things like voice mail password resets…if that would be possible." Paul said, his tone becoming more accommodating.

"It would be. I'm sure there are other simple and repetitive outages that could be handed off to this team as well." Justin added.

"Something to consider, I guess. But listen, I really need to get this work done. You have what you need from me for now?" Paul said.

"Sure, I didn't mean to interrupt your work." Justin said in an apologetic tone.

"That's no problem. Your idea sounds promising and I bet you have others. Listen if you've got other ideas similar to the one you just mentioned; I wouldn't mind hearing about them." Paul said to Justin's surprise.

"Sure. I'll hook up with you after the meeting with the CIO tomorrow and let you know what he had to say."

Paul didn't say anything further but just turned around and continued to work.

Perhaps Paul is on board after all…at least partially with the Service Desk idea. Better than the "Get out of here and let me do my job" he halfway expected to get. With the somewhat successful discussion with Paul in his hip pocket, he thought he'd find Rudy and see how he made out with the Network and Server Teams.

Well, One Out of Three Ain't bad…if you're a Baseball Player

Justin found Rudy heading back to his cube and caught up with him so they could walk together. Justin patted Rudy's back as he caught up with him in the hallway.

"How did you make out with the teams?" Justin asked, hoping for good news.

"Both teams essentially told me to 'go pound sand.'" Rudy said dejectedly.

"Well, I only did slightly better, Paul was nearly ready to tell me the same thing until I threw in the SPOC idea…he mellowed and actually seemed to like the concept."

"Well, where does that leave us?" Rudy inquired.

"I guess it leaves us right where we started and where we thought we were." Justin said.

"And where is that?"

"Working in an IT department that is nothing but a bunch of individual silos all doing their own thing." Justin announced.

"…and apparently happy to keep it that way." Rudy added.

"Yeah, but that's a leadership challenge."

Back at their desks, Justin and Rudy decided to map out the slide presentation they were going to give to Mr. Jones tomorrow afternoon. Justin had in his head how he thought it should play out in front of the CIO.

"How about something like this?" Justin asked of Rudy as he began scribbling out the following:

SLIDE 1—Introduction to the Brief

SLIDE 2—Overview of Lifecycle

SLIDE 3—Incident Management

SLIDE 4—Change Management

SLIDE 5—Service Desk

SLIDE 6—Leadership Role?

Rudy looked at Justin's notes with an inquisitive look on his face. He wasn't quite certain that Justin was done.

"Is that it? There is more to IT Service Management than just this. Even I know that much." Rudy inquired.

"Well, yes, but we don't have time to discuss, or even really evaluate the benefits of everything. This will serve as a jumping off point for the CIO. If we try to get into more than that, we'll be in there for hours…nobody wants that." Justin said smiling.

"I'm with you on that." Rudy replied. "What do you need from me?"

"Can you use this and start putting some draft slides together? I need to better understand the Leadership role in all this...you know the last slide? I need to do a little more research for that piece."

"Sure thing." Rudy responded picking up the piece of paper from Justin's desk and heading back over to his cubicle to start working on the presentation.

Company Leadership—How much involvement is enough?

Justin knew what he was looking for. He knew he had an old book on basic leadership somewhere in his desk. He knew it wouldn't contain much in the way of specifics, but he wanted to make a compelling case to the CIO that company leadership support for any change in the way the IT department currently operates would require the CIO's unwavering support. In addition to being able to refresh himself on the role of leadership in this effort; assuming that the CIO does ultimately approve their recommendations, he thought a few leadership nuggets in the book might be useful for the slide presentation…to emphasize that any significant IT change must have leadership support to be successful.

While Justin was digging through his desk, he decided to take some time to clean up his workspace and get rid of some old items he no longer needed. He pulled out stacks of papers he had stuck in his desk drawers years ago with plans to retain them for some reason, but over time the documents and memos had turned into trash waiting for someone to put them out of their misery and into a shredder. Justin found the leadership book at the bottom of the middle drawer and as he pulled it out, he remembered how large it was…it had to be nearly 500 pages. He landed it on his desk with a loud thud.

"What was that?" Rudy yelled from the adjoining cubicle.

"I found the leadership book I was looking for." Justin responded.

"Hey, keep it down over there. These slides aren't going to create themselves." Rudy joked.

"Sure, didn't realize you needed all your brain power to put a few slides together." Justin jabbed back at his friend. He heard a slight chuckle from his friend.

Justin forgot how large this book was, which probably explained how it came to rest at the bottom of a desk drawer. But he didn't intend to read this book cover to cover, he was only looking for a few small blurbs pertaining to leadership and its role in organizational change. He began looking through the table of contents and something quickly caught his eye: Chapter 7: Organizational Change and Leadership. Scanning the rest of the table of contents he looked for anything else that might be helpful, but didn't find anything useful. He assumed if he were to find anything in this area it would be in chapter 7. He quickly flipped the book to the beginning of the applicable chapter.

Leadership is often an ignored skill in regards to change. Change can be a traumatic exercise for an organization and often create more problems than it solves…"

"Blah, Blah…just fluff." Justin thought as he scanned further down looking for the meat of the chapter.

We all know change is inevitable. Yet in the midst of transformation, too many leaders abdicate. A leader must be strong enough to take charge of the change. The best type of change happens when leaders envision and control the organizational change. That type of change creates opportunities, transforms companies and ignites growth. Otherwise, you're faced with the damaging prospect of change that happens in spite of you, rather than because of you.

First, you need to "define your change" – think expansively about the future and what change you need to undertake. Next, you must "sell your change" to your employees, other leaders and all stakeholders. Often, this isn't easy: Educating employees regarding pending changes prior to implementation can be helpful. Also, involve employees in the change planning and allow positive comments to grow naturally...address negative comments as they arise; not letting them fester and grow into something that can hamper change success. Finally, it's time to execute: Genuine leaders get everyone else to buy in by diving headfirst into the cause and never asking anyone to do anything they wouldn't do themselves. Monitor change success and advertise successes to the organization...this can be a driving force in future change endeavors...we did it before and we can do it again.

"Bingo." Justin thought. This seemed to capture the spirit of leadership and change he was looking for. Plus, he felt confident he could craft a few suitable bullets from this text for the slide on leadership. Justin realized that 30 minutes had passed since he started looking for the leadership book. He wondered how Rudy was progressing with the slides.

Slide Presentation—A Kind Look at our Failures

Justin got up to go over to Rudy's cube to check on his progress in getting the draft slides together.

"How's it coming?" Justin asked as he entered Rudy's cubicle.

"Let me show you what I have so far." Rudy responded.

Rudy clicked through the slides on his computer as Justin stood behind him.

"You know, why not put the slides regarding the Service Desk and Incident Management adjacent to each other since they are related; given that our argument is that the Service Desk will own the incidents." Justin said.

"That's a good idea." Rudy responded quickly moving the slides around on the presentation. "What do you think we should have on the Recommendation Slide?"

Rudy flipped down to the Recommendation slide and Justin observed that it was blank except for the title.

"Well, under the title say…'Quick Win Recommendations.' We want to make sure the CIO understands that this is just the start."

"Good idea." Rudy said typing away.

"Item 1: Service Desk with skillsets from DSS/Voice/Networks/Server teams…something like that."

Rudy hammered away at the keyboard.

"Item 2: Stop the Change bleeding with a Change Management process."

"I like that." Rudy said.

"Item 3: Start actually managing incidents by allowing the SD to own each one." Justin said. "I guess that's about it."

"Put this on the Leadership Slide, will you?" Justin asked, handing a note with some bullets handwritten on it. Rudy looked at it and gave Justin a thumbs up.

Justin stared at the slides a bit longer before having a revelation.

"You know what…instead of only the one slide on the Service Desk…how about this?" Justin said scribbling out a graphic and then doing another one that looked similar but wasn't.

"Oh, I get it. A before and after kind of thing." Rudy said looking at both scribbled graphics.

"Exactly. They say a picture is worth a thousand words…let's find out if that is true." Justin added.

"Okay, give me a few minutes to make the changes and I'll send it to you." Rudy said, returning to his keyboard.

"Okay, while you're working on that I'll knock out a couple of voice mails." He said referring to the customer calls for assistance that were probably waiting for him.

Justin saw his voice mail count was up to 7. He listened to all of them and then got to work addressing each of them. Most of them were easy fixes that he could take care of remotely from his desk, but one of them he knew he'd have to go to the employee's desk to address…no power to the computer. He had the six issues resolved in under 30 minutes then grabbed his tool bag and a spare PC power supply and power cord and headed to the customer's desk.

When he arrived he noticed Melissa Simpson, a Claims Processing Agent, sitting at her desk reading a romance novel.

"Looks like you're dead in the water." Justin said smiling.

"It's about time you got here." She replied curtly.

"We do the best we can…staffing shortage and all." He replied while giving the PC a quick look.

"Well, I can't do my job with a PC that won't turn on. It's your job to fix it, not mine."

Justin was relieved to see that it was just a frayed power cable; that should have been replaced when the new PC was installed during the PC Swap project, but one of his co-workers in DSS must have missed it.

"I think I see the problem…we'll have you fixed in a jiffy." Justin said maintaining his professionalism; pleased that the fix would be a quick one and he wouldn't have to be in Melissa's company any longer than necessary.

Justin unplugged the cable from the back of the PC and the power strip and tossed it into the trash can. After installing the new cord, he plugged it in and the PC sprang back to life initiating its boot sequence.

"There you go. It should be fine now. Let me know if you have any other problems." Justin said as he turned to leave.

"Yeah, you'll be the first one I call." Melissa responded sarcastically.

Ironic Justin thought as he headed back to his cubicle, had there been a Service Desk, she would be calling them; and giving them a hard time, instead of him directly. When he arrived back at his cube, Rudy mentioned that the slides were done and in his inbox.

Justin opened up the email and attachment and began to review the slides…they seemed perfect.

"Okay, I'm going to email the slides to Mrs. Evans in the CIO's office, she'll make sure everything's ready for the meeting tomorrow. I assume we're meeting in the conference room up there." Justin announced.

"Sure. I'm going to take care of a few more calls before I leave for the day." Rudy said.

"Yeah, I've got a couple of new ones, but they can wait until tomorrow. I'm calling it a day; I'll see you tomorrow." Justin said.

Justin got up and headed for the door; knowing he was about as ready as he could be for the meeting with the CIO Mr. Jones tomorrow, but he still felt a twinge of nervousness when he thought about it. He had never been into the CIO's area of the building unless he was there to fix something. Tomorrow he would be there for a very different reason.

'Twas the Night Before the Briefing…and all Through the House

Justin was hoping for a quiet and normal night in stark contrast to what he experienced the night before when he couldn't get his mind off the task of determining if IT Service Management offered any benefits to the company. He so wanted an evening without a work related distraction, he left the manual and the leadership book at work to ensure he wouldn't be drawn to them as he was the manual the evening before. All Justin wanted this evening was some mind-numbing entertainment on television…he didn't even want to watch the news, which was his customary routine.

After unlocking the door to his apartment and entering, he put his backpack down on the kitchen counter and draped his lightweight jacket over a chair by the counter. Oddly, he wasn't very hungry and decided a bowl of cereal would suffice for the evening meal. He looked in the cupboard and pulled out a box of Count Chocula. Justin had long since given up trying to choke down the more healthy cereal for the kind with an un-holy quantity of sugar added. He didn't eat cereal all that often, so he figured it wasn't all that bad.

With his cereal bowl spilling over with chocolate cereal and marshmallow shapes, he made his way to the sofa and clicked on the television. Time to do a little channel surfing…staying away from the news stations, of course. After a few minutes he settled on a rerun of "Mr. Belvedere," a show about an English butler that works for a dysfunctional family in Pittsburg. Speaking of dysfunctional, Mr. Belvedere could work for our IT department, he thought. While watching the show, he recalled how the show centered mostly on the "Wesley" character; a young boy that seemed to have a knack for getting into trouble and causing a great deal of grief for everyone, especially Mr. Belvedere.

"Man, that character is a real piece of work." Justin said to himself in response to some mischievous act by Wesley. Justin even found himself chuckling a bit to certain parts of the show. Right now, the briefing to the CIO was the last thing on his mind. As the final credits began to run, Justin's cell phone rang and he saw on the caller ID that it was Rudy.

"Hello?" Justin said into his phone as he answered.

"I've got some news for you that I thought you'd want to know before tomorrow." Rudy responded.

"Just when I was starting to forget all about this briefing stuff…" Justin thought to himself.

"What is it?" Justin inquired.

"Mrs. Evans called from the CIO office to say she got the slides okay." Rudy responded.

"Okay, that's good."

"Yeah, but that's not all. She also told me the brief was moved up to 10 AM to accommodate a few others that will attend." Rudy said, unintentionally building the suspense.

"Who else?" Justin asked.

"The company president and a couple of board members."

There was silence between them for a few seconds that seemed like an eternity.

"Are you still there?" Rudy finally asked.

"Yeah, I'm still here. Wow, I didn't expect this." Justin said, finally understanding the importance of the briefing was kicked up a notch now that more higher ups were also going to be in attendance.

"What should we do…anything?" Rudy asked.

"Well, I think we were prepared for the CIO, but I have no idea what these other folks might be interested in. Could be a game changer, but I don't think we can do anything about it now. All we can do is go as planned and hope we don't look like idiots if the president or a board member asks us something we don't know."

"I guess you're right about that." Rudy responded.

"I tell you what…bring a copy of the slides to breakfast in the morning and we'll do a quick run through to make sure we have all the facts in place." Justin suggested.

"Okay, will do. I'm going to go home and throw up." Rudy said jokingly, but clearly his nerves had kicked into gear.

"Hey, what's the worst that can happen?"

"We could look like morons and get fired."

"Oh yeah. I guess we just need to be the smartest two in the conference room tomorrow." Justin said.

After they hung up, Rudy presumably went to empty his belly of his lunch time meal while Justin returned to another episode of "Mr. Belvedere." But this time although his eyes were fixed on the television screen, his didn't see a thing. His mind was playing mental images of the conference room, its attendees, and tomorrow's briefing. Justin and Rudy would both have a difficult time falling

asleep this night.

Briefing Day & the Brain Bladder Conundrum

As Justin entered the cafeteria the following morning, he spotted Rudy in the back corner by a window. Rudy wore a sports jacket with open collar and a nice pair of Dockers; a significant step up from the jeans and polo shirt he normally wore. As Justin approached Rudy, he spread his arms as if to acknowledge his wardrobe choice for the day.

"Great minds think alike, I guess." Justin said referring to his similar attire.

Rudy looked up from the briefing slides but said nothing. Then he turned his attention back to the slides he printed out the day before.

"So what's wrong?" Justin inquired, sensing his friend was troubled.

"Man, aren't you worried about how this will go? I mean, the president of the company for crying out loud." Rudy exclaimed, raising his voice more than he should.

Justin pulled out a chair and took a seat next to Rudy.

"Look, just take it easy. They put their pants on the same as you and me." Justin said.

"Yeah, but they don't buy their pants at Wal-Mart."

Justin just chuckled. He placed his hand on Rudy's shoulder in an attempt to calm him down. Justin would need Rudy during the briefing. Rudy had good ideas and his comments would be an important part of the overall effectiveness of the briefing.

"Let me buy you a coffee…it will steady your nerves." Justin suggested.

"No thanks. I've felt like I needed to pee ten times already this morning." Rudy said continuing to study the slides.

"Dude, that's just the brain/bladder conundrum…it's just nerves." Justin laughed. "Listen, I'll be doing most of the talking, all you have to do is run the PC and step through the briefing slides as we go along. If you have something to say…chime in. That doesn't sound so bad, right?"

"I guess not." Rudy replied looking up from the slides.

"Okay, now how about that coffee?"

"Sure, but you better make it a small." Rudy responded with a smile.

Justin got up to get the coffee as Rudy returned to the slides that sat on the table in front of him. He was beginning to feel better about the upcoming briefing; especially since Justin had just informed him that he would be doing most of the talking and all Rudy would have to do is to operate the computer and manage the slide show. In his mind, he now figured it wouldn't be that bad.

Within a few minutes, Justin returned with the coffee and sat back down next to Rudy.

"So, you think we're ready...couple of hours before we need to be upstairs." Justin said, referring to the CIO's conference room.

"Yeah, I think so; like you said, we have no idea what the board members or the company president might ask, so we'll just have to play it by ear." Rudy responded, clearly feeling less nervous than before; as he took a sip of his coffee.

"I think we're good to go as well; we might as well head downstairs while we wait, we can knock out a few customer calls." Justin responded, wanting to find a productive way to kill some time before the briefing.

As they both walked out of the cafeteria heading to their cubicles, Justin glanced back at the table he was sitting at when the CIO first approached him. He noticed someone else sitting there this morning and he wondered who they were and how this person's day would map out. He didn't recognize the person, but she was dressed very well; especially for around here he thought. He just figured she was an "early morning" sales rep making a pitch of some kind or other to someone at the insurance company. At this particular moment, all Justin knew was that she was attractive and clearly out of place. Justin would not have to wait long to discover who this woman was and why she was here today.

As Rudy walked by the entrance to the cafeteria, he tossed his still nearly full coffee into the nearest trash bin.

Killing Time on DSS Drive

As Justin and Rudy arrived at the DSS area down in the basement, they immediately saw Steve doing his best "Lumbergh" act from the movie "Office Space." With coffee cup in hand he was chatting with one of the other DSS agents as they arrived at their desk. When Steve saw Justin and Rudy arrive, dressed better than normal, he headed directly toward them.

"You guys are dressed to impress, I see." Steve said casually.

"We figured if the company president and a couple of board members were going to be there too, we better look a little better than jeans and a polo shirt." Rudy replied.

"I heard Mr. Ferguson was going to be there...which board members are attending?" Steve inquired.

"No clue." Rudy answered. "When Mrs. Evans from the CIO's office called to tell me about the additions to the briefing, she didn't say who on the board would attend."

"Boys, it probably doesn't matter. Doubt anyone on the board or even the president knows much about how the IT department here operates anyway. I suspect that Mr. Jones has confidence in what you two will say and wants Mr. Ferguson and the board members to hear it."

This statement, coming from someone the boys were clearly beginning to admire carried more weight than it would have a few days earlier. Justin and Rudy had had more interaction with Steve in the last few days than in the previous few months. Both began to develop more respect for Steve.

"Did you get the final slides up to the CIO's office for the brief?" Steve inquired.

"Yeah, they got them." Justin responded.

"You mind if I take a look?" Steve inquired.

"Yeah, I got a copy right here." Rudy responded holding the briefing slides up.

"Let's take a look in my office." Steve said motioning the two to follow him to his office.

When they got to his office, Steve went behind his desk and motioned to Justin and Rudy to take a seat. The two sat down just as they did when they were gathering data from Steve earlier in their quest.

"Let's have a look." Steve said; his hand extended requesting the slides from Rudy.

Steve looked over the slides while Justin and Rudy sat quietly, hoping Steve didn't find anything significantly bad in anything they planned to present. Steve's opinion now meant more to them than either would have thought a few days earlier. Steve took an extraordinarily long time reviewing the slides...clearly giving each slide considerable thought as he flipped through them all. After he flipped through the last slide, Steve straightened out the briefing slides and slid them across the desk back to Rudy.

"These look pretty darn good guys." Steve said with a smile.

"I hope the big wigs think so too." Justin answered.

"No matter how it goes, you did what the CIO requested...no one can take that away from you regardless of how it goes. You both should be proud of that." Steve said offering some encouraging words.

"We appreciate that." Rudy said looking over to Justin who nodded in agreement.

It was now nearly 9:30AM and neither Justin nor Rudy wanted to wait around another 30 minutes before heading up to the conference room. As luck would have it, Samantha, another DSS technician, came into Steve's office with some news.

"Excuse me guys, but Mrs. Evans just called and said they are ready upstairs and you guys can head up early if you want…which I took to mean you guys need to come up there now." She said, nearly out of breath as she likely ran from her desk to deliver the message.

"Well, it looks like it's Showtime." Steve commented in regards to Samantha's news. "You guys want me to go with you?"

"We got it…right, Rudy?" Justin said with confidence.

"Not a problem." Rudy responded his nerves now well in check.

Justin and Rudy rose to make their way up to the CIO's office and specifically the conference room. Both were now looking forward to the opportunity and felt confident in their preparation.

The Briefing—Showtime

As Justin and Rudy stepped off the elevator on the CIO Office floor, they saw Mrs. Evans sitting at her desk outside of the CIO conference room at the end of the long hallway. As Rudy made his way down the long hallway with Justin by his side, he couldn't help but have a "Green Mile" flashback as though he was walking the last of many steps leading to the electric chair. But, with a muffled chuckle, he quickly cast that thought out of his mind. Mrs. Evans didn't look up from her work until both Justin and Rudy were nearly to her desk.

"Everyone is in the conference room waiting on you. Go on in." She said without looking up; yet pointing to the closed conference room door.

"Well, you ready to get this over with?" Justin asked.

Rudy said nothing, but the confident expression on his face spoke volumes as he opened the door and allowed Justin to enter first. Rudy followed quickly behind and closed the door behind them.

Upon entering they immediately saw the first slide prepped on the screen at the front of the conference room.

IT Service Management's Applicability to the Southern United Insurance Company

PRESENTED BY JUSTIN SMITH & RUDY VARGAS

Jackson Jones, the CIO and J. Roth Ferguson, the Company President sat on opposite sides of the long conference room table toward the front of the screen where the briefing slides would be displayed. Sitting on either side were two other people, one Justin immediately recognized. She was the person sitting down in the cafeteria he noticed earlier. She sat on the same side of the table as the President while the other person sat next to the CIO. The PC that operated the slides was at the opposite end of the table and it was clear Justin and Rudy were to sit at the far end of the table to conduct the briefing.

"Thank you for joining us this morning." Mr. Jones stated, breaking the ice. "Please have a seat and I'll introduce everyone."

Justin and Rudy sat down with Rudy sitting behind the computer. Justin adjusted some notes he had brought with him but basically planned to conduct the brief from what was on the slides.

"This is Mr. J. Ross Ferguson, our Company President." The CIO began.

Mr. Ferguson was a rather rotund individual with a graying almost white beard and long white hair. Had he been wearing a red suit he would certainly have been hounded by star struck children mistaking him for Santa Claus. In this case, he was wearing a gray three piece suit. When his introduction was made, he only briefly looked up to see the newcomers in the room. He seemed to have an interest in being elsewhere.

"Additionally, we have Ms Tabitha Carson and Mr. James Walton, two of our company Board Members. Looking toward Justin and Rudy, the CIO now introduced the two that would present the briefing. President Ferguson looked at his watch as if to signal to get on with the briefing as he was tiring of the niceties.

"I believe I saw you two in the cafeteria this morning." Tabitha chimed in. She was young for a board member...at least that was Justin's first impression. She was impeccably dressed and her blond hair was tied up and sat neatly on top of her head without a strand out of place.

"Yes ma'am. I thought I noticed you as well. I wondered who you were. You seemed a bit out of place." Justin replied. Tabitha smiled back at Justin and Rudy.

"Listen folks, can we get on with it? I have a busy day ahead of me." The President broke in. Without another word, Rudy moved the presentation to the next slide. Justin took Rudy's action as a call to start the briefing.

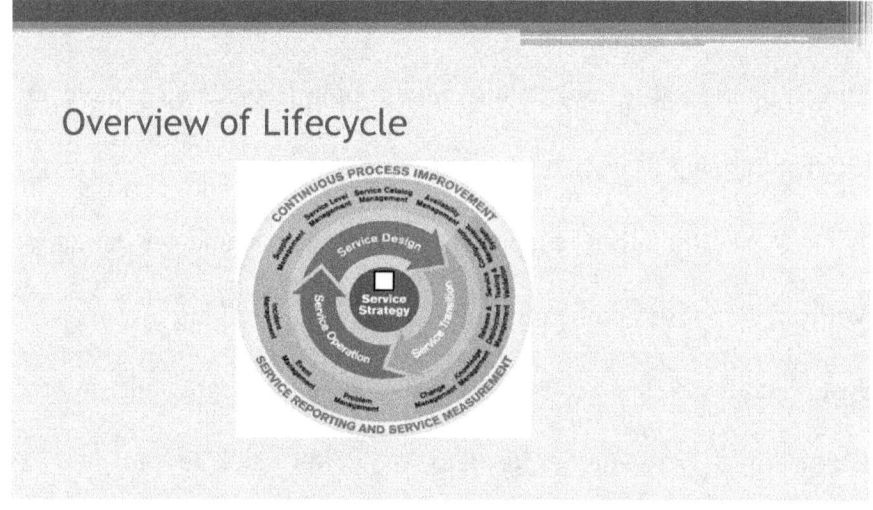

Overview of Lifecycle

"As Mr. Jones may have mentioned, he asked us to evaluate the applicability of IT management concepts within our company and specifically the IT department's current processes." Justin started the briefing. In a very high level method, he described the 5 parts of the IT Service Management concept.

As he concluded and was about to move on to the next slide, Ms Carson chimed in.

"I may have missed this, but why were you two asked to do this?" She inquired looking primarily toward the CIO.

"Justin is one of the very few that actually has had some training in this area." Mr. Jones responded to her question.

"Okay, I understand." She responded, as she scribbled a few notes. With that, Rudy advanced the presentation to the next slide.

Incident Management (IM)

- Definition—an incident is an unplanned interruption to an IT service or a reduction in the quality of that service. IM's primary objective is to resume the regular state of affairs as quickly as possible and to minimize the impact to business processes.
- Who owns IT outages here? (currently the customer/employee experiencing the outage)
- Who should own IT outages here? (???)

Justin continued.

"With so much encompassing the breadth and depth of this, we found a few concepts that we believe can be a more immediate benefit to us. One in particular is Incident Management." Justin explained.

"What are we currently doing in regards to this Incident Management area?" Mr. Walton, the other Board Member inquired.

"Essentially, we're not using any formal Incident Management process." Rudy responded to Justin's surprise.

"You see, currently when someone in the office has a problem with their computer, for example, they call one of the IT sections to try to get someone to work the problem. Eventually they get someone to work it; often after more than one call. For example, let's say an employee thinks their PC is the issue, they might call us in DSS…if it turns out to be a server or network problem, they have delayed the fix action by not knowing who to call to work the problem. This results in frustration for the employee and lost productivity for the company because action needed to resolve the issue is delayed." Justin explained

"That's not good, Jackson. How do we fix that? Lost productivity is also lost revenue." President Ferguson said, finally keying in on something he knew the shareholders would be concerned about. The CIO looked over to Justin and Rudy hoping they had a suitable response.

"That's a good question sir. We believe a Service Desk is the answer to that problem." Rudy said as he moved the presentation on to the next slide.

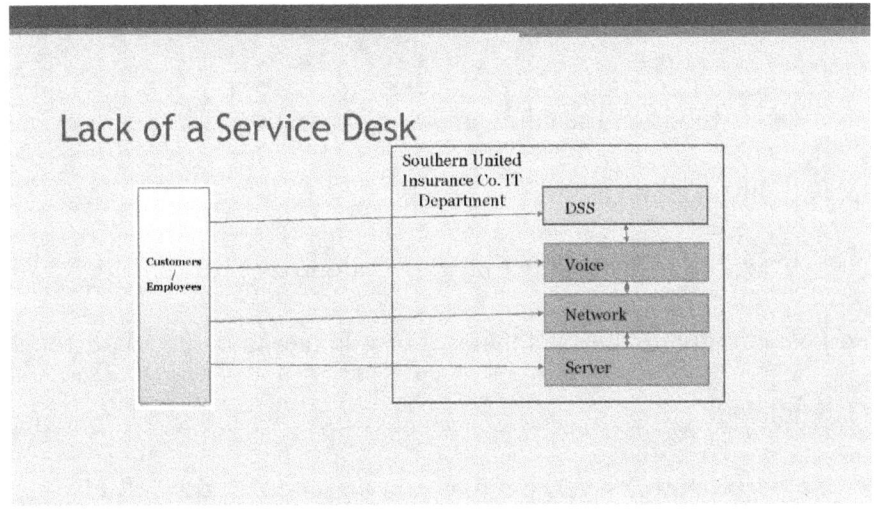

"You see..." Justin continued. "...this is where we are now. Customers/employees must figure out; or own their issue, until they can find someone in the IT department to essentially work their problem. This method costs the company productivity and money."

"Okay, what's this Service Desk thing you mentioned?" Tabitha inquired.

Service Desk

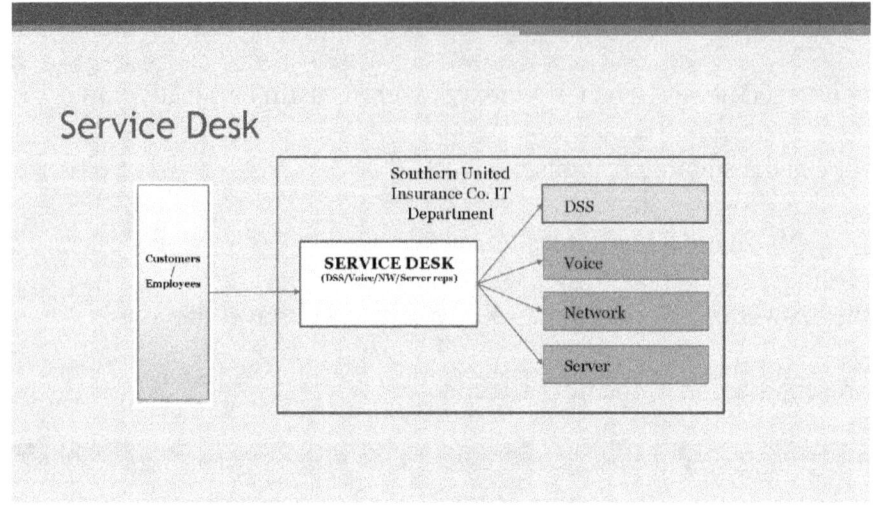

"Here you can see the same thing but now with a Service Desk." Justin pointed out.

"Isn't this just another layer in our current process?" Mr. Ferguson inquired. "Won't that just take longer to fix an employee's IT problem?"

"It's another layer, but there are definite benefits." Rudy said.

"Exactly…" Justin continued. "…notice in the Service Desk box there is representation from the other IT sections. Additionally, there is only one entity the customers now need to call or interact with. One customer phone call and the Service Desk now own the customer's problem. It is there, within the Service Desk, where many problems can be solved without even going to the individual IT departments."

"I have to admit…I don't really understand." Tabitha Carson stated.

"Okay, let's say a customer has a problem. They call the Service Desk, regardless of what the problem's ultimate root cause might be. The Service Desk is then responsible to assign the problem to the appropriate level technician with the right skillset to fix the customer's problem. Again, in many cases problems will be fixed at the Service Desk level…resulting in a faster resolution with no disruption to any IT department."

"Ok, so what do the members of the actual IT sections do now?" Mr. Jones inquired.

"That's the other good thing about a Service Desk. The higher skilled techs in the sections are left to work more complicated problems the Service Desk can't handle. When one that fits this criterion comes to the Service Desk, they know which IT section to pass it to. These higher skilled techs can spend their time on more complicated issues rather than be overwhelmed with easy to fix customer problems."

Justin and Rudy saw engagement and approval from the leadership in the conference room. Neither of them really expected them, save for the CIO, to show this much interest.

"I can't speak for the rest of the group, but you've certainly gotten my attention." Mr. Walton said. "What else have you got to show us?"

"Great. Let's talk Change Management for a few minutes. I think you'll see there are benefits to be gained here as well." Justin said, motioning for Rudy to move to the next slide in the presentation.

Acting on Justin's recommendation, Rudy advanced the slide to the next one in the deck—Change Management. The leadership in the conference room read through the slide before Justin continued, each apparently eager to learn how this could benefit the company as much as it appeared an Incident Management process and a Service Desk would.

Change Management

- A CHANGE is defined as a modification or removal of authorized, planned or supported services or service components and its associated documentation.
- Types of changes:
- Routine—pose little risk and are pre-authorized (password resets/PC upgrades/etc.)
  - (Self Service Changes)
- Emergency—has a significant impact on the business and is often in response to a failure

- Example of a failed change: *the past customer PC swap*

"Okay, again I'm curious as to how we're handling changes currently?" The company president inquired after looking the change slide over for a few minutes.

"Therein lies the problem as we were able to determine. We don't really know for certain what, if any, process exists for doing changes." Rudy responded.

"Exactly, Rudy…" Justin quickly chimed in before more questions could be asked. "…we suspect that whenever something needs to change…software upgrade to a server, or IOS upgrade to a network device, the IT team in charge of that proceeds with the change when it is convenient for them to do it."

"And that works to a point, correct?" The CIO questioned.

"Certainly, however, one of the pieces that is missing is a proper accountability for how a change impacts others. Let's say the network team needs to upgrade a router's IOS software due to a security vulnerability that CISCO put out...pretty important and needs to be done right away, correct?" Justin questions.

Everyone, except Rudy, nodded in agreement.

"But when should it be done? Is it permissible to do it during the middle of the day when the claims department is processing on-line insurance premiums or processing claims from customers? Perhaps so. But, will this change isolate the claims department from the network while the change is being done? What happens if something goes horribly wrong during the change? Can the change be backed out?" Justin inquired.

"Hold on there, young fella." The Kris Kringle looking company president said jumping in. "Can you rein in that horse just a bit? You're throwing a lot at us pretty fast."

Justin realized that he was on a bit of a roll and was throwing rhetorical questions at them left and right. He needed to slow it down just a bit so the leadership could get a clear picture. He took a short breath and began again.

"Sorry, all I'm saying is that any change must be assessed as to the impact on the organization as a whole, the business impact; not just whether it is convenient for the team that is doing the change to do it at 3PM on a Friday, because no one wants to stay late to get it done after normal business hours when business impact and risk are minimal. All significant changes should be approved by a Change Board made up of all appropriate stakeholders that potentially could be impacted by the change. If the board doesn't approve the change, then the change doesn't proceed until the board's concerns are addressed." Justin said to hopefully clarify.

"Hey Justin, the failed PC Swap." Rudy pointed out.

"I was going to ask what that was." Tabitha stated pointing to the last bullet on the change slide.

"A few months ago a decision was made to swap out nearly everyone's PC with a new one. On the surface it's certainly a good thing to do to get everyone using new and more robust computing hardware. A pretty significant company-wide change, to be sure. But here was the problem from a DSS perspective and where the train went off the tracks a bit. When we got our lists of PCs to swap out and took the new PCs to the users to replace the old for the new one, not one employee had any idea we were coming. In most cases we either had to wait for them to finish what they were doing before we could begin or had to come back at a later date…again wasted time for DSS and the user."

"Also, once the PCs were swapped out, many users no longer had specialty software needed to do their jobs. There was only one build done for the replacement PCs. So, the DSS folks had to go back and install various kinds of software on employee's new machines." Rudy said adding a point that he thought Justin forgot.

"Yeah, I almost forgot that. Thanks Rudy. Had this change been properly vetted, the need for multiple builds would have come up and been addresses beforehand. For example, perhaps there would have been a 'Claims Build' PC earmarked to replace an old PC in the Claims department. This new PC would have been pre-loaded with all the specialty software Claims personnel need to do their jobs. The swap could have been as simple as a plug and play action." Justin stated.

Even though Justin and Rudy were not speaking very well of the current conditions of the IT department; something for which the CIO was the senior leader, once he finished this last statement he noticed that the CIO just gave both of them a "thumbs up" with an added smile of approval. This confused both Justin and Rudy; but they assumed the CIO would clue them in later.

"These are certainly some good ideas you boys have come up with. What else do you have for us?" Mr. Ferguson asked.

With that Rudy moved the presentation to the next slide on leadership.

Leadership Role

- *"...any significant organizational change will require consistent and unyielding support at the highest levels of the organization..."*
- "...employee buy-in to any organizational shift or change can be aided by employee education prior to the change taking place..."
- "...set up a company-wide advertisement plan for the change..."
- "...information flow in regards to a significant organizational change must be free to flow bi-directionally..."
- "Where there is no vision, the people perish"
  - --Proverbs

"We wanted something to emphasize how important leadership is in any change to the way an organization conducts business. In retrospect, I suppose you already know this, but here are just some quotes to further drive the idea home. If you want to go forward with anything we've discussed here, it needs to be driven from the top down with unwavering support. There will always be

some level of resistance to change." Justin explained.

"Not my first rodeo, son. We get that…that's why we are

here." The company president said, speaking on behalf of the others

at the table. Rudy quickly moved on to the last slide in the

presentation.

Recommendation/Conclusions

- --Quick Win Recommendations
  - --SERVICE DESK comprised of skillsets from DSS/Voice/Network/Server (lower level skillsets)
  - --Stop the change bleeding with a Change Management Process.
  - --Start actually managing Incidents…allow Service Desk to own every Incident.

"So, there is a lot more to IT and Service Management than

what we've talked about here this morning; but we wanted to discuss

only areas we thought could be quicker wins that would show some

defined benefits." Justin explained. "So, we recommend the

following 3 items for your consideration: An IT Service Desk,

Define a universal Change Management process, and start managing incidents where the Service Desk owns the incident from cradle to grave."

Justin paused here to allow the concepts to percolate just a bit. Nods of approval were evident in the room by all in attendance. Rudy flipped to the last slide that asked the group for questions; which both Justin and Rudy expected.

Questions?

Justin and Rudy could see that everyone was shifting through the notes they took and racking their brains to decide what question or concern needed to be verbalized. For a few brief moments it seemed like the end of one of those briefings where no questions were asked and everyone just wanted to depart. Justin and Rudy knew that often meant the subject of the briefing would be forgotten the moment those in attendance departed the conference room. They both hoped that wasn't the case and were actually glad when Mr. Walton broke the ice.

"Gentlemen, this is fascinating stuff you have presented here this morning. I do have a question for you regarding your Service Desk concept." He announced.

"Yes sir?" Justin replied.

"Funding…should we assume that in order to make this Service Desk a reality, we would need to fund additional billets and added IT hardware; not to mention a place somewhere in the building to work out of?" Mr. Walton inquired.

Justin knew the issue of funding the costs of some of these recommendations would come up so he wasn't surprised when it did. He was, however a bit taken aback when Rudy quickly began to answer Mr. Walton's question.

"There is always going to be some start-up costs with a new venture like this, but long term benefits can be realized. We haven't done any analysis as to what it would cost or what the ROI would be…"

ROI? Justin thought. He wasn't even aware that Rudy knew what ROI meant. Rudy must have been holding out on him—knowledge wise. Justin decided to chime in since he anticipated this question and had a more palatable short term solution in mind.

"There is a short term solution we can employ rather quickly. Use existing resources by taking one person from each IT section within the company and assign them to the new Service Desk. There is some unused space adjacent to the current DSS section and we could build four cubicles there. We'd still need to run some phone and network lines…we could do that. Basically, the entire build of the Service Desk would be run like any other project here. Two other things we would need to work out would be developing a process for how the Service Desk interacts with the other IT Sections; and deciding how to announce this change to the workforce." Justin said, fully knowing that there would be hundreds of other large and minute details that would need to be addressed before the concept became a reality.

"So, based on what you mentioned previously, the lesser skilled techs would staff the Service Desk." Mr. Walton inquired.

"That was my thought. These folks are used to handling the easier day to day issues that come up and it would free the higher skilled techs to work the more challenging jobs." Justin responded.

"You know, there is some benefit to setting up some sort of rotational opportunity for all IT personnel to work in the Service Desk." Rudy chimed in. "This gives all IT folks an opportunity to appreciate the power of the Service Desk in providing our customers service. It really depends on the direction the company leadership wants to go."

"Excellent thought, Rudy…" Tabitha Carson said now jumping into the conversation. "…but I'm intrigued by this Change Management concept. I like actually managing changes to our infrastructure, but Justin there never seems to be a good time to do a change that doesn't impact someone; unless the person does it during midnight on a Saturday. I don't like forcing someone to work over the weekend. Are there another options to getting these needed changes done?"

Here was a question that Justin hadn't anticipated. He knew something would come up that they weren't prepared for. He thought for a few seconds and then an idea began to formulate in his head.

"Ms Carson, that's a challenge to be sure…" He started.

"Please call me Tabitha." She interjected.

"Of course…Tabitha. What we could do would be to establish a Standard Maintenance Window. This is an established timeframe every week or every other week where we've determined maintenance actions will be the least disruptive and present the lowest risk. Changes would still need to be approved but the Change Board would need to encourage changes to be conducted during this window unless a compelling reason not to is presented."

"Excellent response, Justin. Thank you very much." Tabitha responded.

Rudy thought he was imagining things, but did Ms. Carson just wink at Justin? Certainly not, he thought to himself. She was a Company Board Member and Justin was just an IT flunky like himself. Rudy was convinced it must have been his imagination or a trick of light and shadow somehow caused by the room projector.

"Any other questions or concerns?" Rudy stated when he saw the conversation between Ms. Carson and Justin had concluded.

"Jackson, I would say that you selected two pretty good candidates to handle this tasking for you." Mr. Ferguson announced, clearly pleased by what was presented. "It sounds like you have some work to do to get your IT house in order."

"I agree with you on both counts, sir." The CIO quickly responded. "If there are no further questions for the boys here, I'll walk them out and we can discuss this further."

When there appeared to be no further questions everyone rose and the company leadership approached Justin and Rudy to shake their hands and congratulate them on the outstanding job in putting the presentation together. Rudy observed that when Ms. Carson shook Justin's hand it was just slightly longer than it needed to be…again it must be his imagination, he surmised.

The CIO, Mr. Jones, escorted the guys out to the hallway while the company leadership remained behind in the conference room. Both Rudy and Justin wondered what Mr. Jones really thought of their findings.

"Thanks to you both." He said with a pat on the back to both of them. "Expect a little something extra in your pay for putting this together. I don't think this could have gone any better."

"Better?" Justin said in surprise. "We kind of slammed our own IT department in there. I figured you'd be a little upset, since you're the CIO of the IT department."

"Look fellas, I came to this position from HR. I sort of wanted a new challenge. I knew the IT department was a bit of a mess when I took the job. What I need is sharp guys like you with ideas on how to fix it. What you did in there was start a conversation along with provide a roadmap to follow to go down a better path...so, like I said, it couldn't have gone any better."

As Mr. Jones turned to reenter the conference room, Justin turned to Rudy.

"You ready for a LARGE coffee now?"

"Sure, if you're buying..." Rudy responded as they both headed for the cafeteria.

"Say, was that Ms. Carson hitting on you or what?" Rudy asked Justin with a chuckle.

Justin's face was filled with a dumbfounded confusion.

"What?" He replied louder than it needed to be.

Hey, Here Comes Your Girlfriend!

As Justin and Rudy made their way to the cafeteria, Justin couldn't help but think about what Rudy said regarding Tabitha. When they got down to the cafeteria, both headed for the Dunkin Donuts which served the best coffee available in the place. Each got a coffee and grabbed one of the few remaining breakfast sandwiches and Justin paid the cashier, as usual.

"How about over there?" Justin inquired to Rudy.

Rudy nodded in agreement and they both headed over to a table in the corner. Since the briefing began early and only lasted 45 minutes or so, it was just now approaching 11:00 AM and the breakfast crowd had thinned out and the lunch rush hadn't begun yet. So, there were very few people in the cafeteria. Rudy sat facing the cafeteria entrance and Justin sat opposite him toward the window.

"Sounds like Mr. Jones was pretty happy with how things went, huh?" Justin said as he began to eat his breakfast sandwich.

"Yeah, I wonder what kind of bonus in our pay he was referring to?" Rudy wondered.

"What difference does it make? Hell, I buy your meals all the time anyway, what do you need with a bonus? I need a bonus just to keep you fed." Justin said as both exchanged laughter partly in relief that the briefing went well but more importantly because it was over.

"Do you really think there will be any changes made in the way we do business around here now?" Rudy questioned to Justin.

"Well, I guess that is hard to say. They seemed pretty interested in some of the concepts we brought up."

"It will be interesting to see what…" Rudy started before stopping abruptly. "…hold the phone, I see your girlfriend coming into the cafeteria."

"What are you talking about?" Justin said.

"Ms. Carson just walked in and she's headed this way." Rudy said. "I'll get another sandwich and give you two lovebirds some privacy."

"Shut up." Justin shot off as Rudy rose to head back to the serving line.

"Justin, I'm glad I caught you." Tabitha announced as she approached the table where Justin sat.

"Oh, hi Ms. Carson." Justin returned politely.

"I asked you to call me Tabitha. I know I'm a board member and all, but honestly, it wasn't all that long ago when I was where you are in your career." She replied. "I caught a few breaks and things just worked out."

"Okay Tabitha, so how did the after meeting go when Rudy and I departed?" Justin was curious to find out.

"Well, you know Mr. Ferguson isn't just the company president, he is also the Chairman of the Board. So, basically for all company board matters, he's my boss."

"I wasn't aware of that, but that makes sense." Justin replied.

"It's a bit odd, me being on the board and all and not being a full time employee, but he wants me to manage a project to stand up a Service Desk here." She announced. "And I think I'm going to need your help since you and Rudy know the ins and outs of this place better than I do."

"We'd love to help." Rudy suddenly announced coming back from getting another breakfast sandwich; apparently using his own money for a change.

"Oh, hi Rudy…good job up there this morning. I was just telling Justin…"

"Yes, I heard. Sounds great." Rudy jumped in.

"Well, I'll leave you both to your meals. Mr. Jones gave me your contact information. Once we get the ball rolling I'll be in contact. Here is my card...my cell is on the back." She said, sliding the business card across the table to Justin. Unexpectedly, she grabbed Justin's hand and gave it a quick squeeze.

"I look forward to working with you...you both...on this exciting effort." She said as she got up to depart. As she was leaving the cafeteria, she glanced over her shoulder in the direction of Justin and Rudy but continued out of the cafeteria.

"What's up with that? Why didn't I get a business card? Oh yeah, I'm not her boyfriend." Rudy joked.

"Cut it out! Listen, the card is for both of us...she didn't need to give us both one." Justin said trying to explain her actions.

"Dude, she is so into you and you don't even realize it." Rudy said. "I'm guessing we'll be seeing more of Tabitha, huh?"

"I guess so. Sounds like she's interested in getting this Service Desk project moving, certainly." Justin said.

"Well, if she can do that…with our help…she has my vote. That would be a benefit for everyone that works here; not just the IT department." Rudy said while taking the last bite of his sandwich.

"Well, I guess we better get back to the office. I'm sure we have lots of voice messages waiting on us." Justin announced, while starting to wonder if there was anything to Rudy's comments concerning Tabitha's interest in him. He quickly surmised whether true or not he would find out in due course. And any romantic opportunities would be secondary to the effort to improve the IT department by instituting a Service Desk.

"If this project is successful, maybe not for much longer." Rudy responded, referring to the tiresome and constant voice messages the DSS folks deal with all the time in handling customer's computer problems.

Justin and Rudy walked a bit taller on the way back to their cubicles as they both felt a sense of pride in what they had accomplished and started for the betterment of the company's IT department and other company employees. They knew much work was ahead for them and others in making their recommendations a reality, but the seedlings of a better and more cohesive IT department had been planted and Justin and Rudy would now be looked to as the primary gardeners of those seeds.

Conclusion and "Almost" Final Thoughts

Justin and Rudy are feeling pretty good about themselves now but their journey to a better IT department is really just beginning. There will be much to accomplish to build out a Service Desk from nothing and both will be in the thick of that struggle. In the next installment of the "Justin and Rudy" series we'll look at the struggles, challenges, and failures they encounter as project members tasked with building the company's Service Desk. We'll look at the project problems that ensue when the project champion, Tabitha Carson becomes an "absent" champion and the struggles Justin and Rudy experience in working with a newly hired project manager with little knowledge of the organization. It's sure to be a bumpy ride for Justin and Rudy; but what IT Adventure isn't a little bumpy on the road to success?

Acknowledgements & Sources:

I would like to thank Lew Kelsey and Kelly Nietubyc for their assistance in editing the often disjointed thoughts and words I call "writing."

ITIL Lifecycle figure from Syntel. (2012). *Application Management Strategic & Consultancy Service.*

Deming Cycle figure taken from Zwetsloot, G. (2003, May 3). From Management Systems to Corporate Responsibility. *Journal of Business Ethics.*

7 Step CSI Process figure taken from Bhardwah, P. (2009 November 25). *You Can't Improve it, if You are not Measureing It.*

FEEL FREE TO POST COMMENTS ON MY AUTHOR'S PAGE: **amazon.com/author/michaelacton**